THE PILOT HOUSE

The Pilot House

poems

David Rigsbee

Black Lawrence Press

Black Lawrence Press
www.blacklawrence.com

Executive Editor: Diane Goettel
Book Design: Steven Seighman

Cover image: "War Dead" by Jill Bullitt

Copyright © 2011 David Rigsbee

Black Lawrence Press
115 Center Ave.
Aspinwall, PA 15215
U.S.A.

Published 2011 by Black Lawrence Press, a division of Dzanc Books

First edition 2011
ISBN: 978-0-9826364-7-3

Printed in the United States

CONTENTS

to Jill and Makaiya

After Reading

I put down the book thinking
how purity is a curse, how it
puts us off the human
for whom it better fits
to turn away from the shore
in favor of the garbage and the grief.
I remember standing in the nave of St. Peter's
looking at the smooth, dead body of Christ
held in Mary's arms and secretly admiring
the madman whose hammer
chipped the same marble that made
Michaelangelo such a monster.

Patience

He knew the chorus and later,
learned the other dances.
Large ships no longer outside his life
looked set free, their reflections
as majestic as their bodies. He knew
that lapping and the beach smell,
the water coming ashore as seabirds
waited, spending their brief lives
in patient attending. *Pazienza*, said the sign
as he entered the library, handing
the librarian a slip of paper
for a poet so long dead that stars
were different when he looked up,
that his language died, waiting for the new stars.

Lincoln

Hanging from the tip of Lincoln's nose,
Cary Grant had one second of the sensation
that draws the swallows to a height
where they no longer have that wing-skate
propulsion through layers but glide
like their distant cousins, the buzzards,
stirring the sky between cloud and corpse.
As perspectives go, it's hard to argue
with circle and sweep, and at intervals
they let go a steely peep, the way a nickel
dropped from the Empire State Building
hits the pavement harmlessly between
taxis: one in use; the other going uptown
beyond the river, into the private streets.

The Gulf

Back in the day you could lie in bed
until the sun had punched through
the low, graphite cloud cover and been
well on the way to its own personal best
and still get a day's work done. Tragedy
went with indolence; loss was all-providing.
You could stand in front of the Easter
Island slab of an ATM and get meaning.
You could toast the air, never worrying
whether a beloved could occupy the same space.
That was the morning, when the river
decided to give itself up to the gulf.
When the riverboat hand, eyeing
the swells, called up to the wheelhouse,
saying, "Cap, are you seeing this?"

He Wondered about the Women

He wondered about the women,
and it seemed to him the past
was like a well in a child's dream.
How was it they managed to keep falling
never to land, never to be stopped,
only getting smaller and smaller?
He was lying on the floor curled up,
his hands holding on to his kneecaps.
"Raise first the knee," the instructor said,
"then the foot higher than the knee.
What does the head do, relative
to the hip?" Peering through
his legs he noticed the instructor
had gone unshaven for several days.
Then everything was quiet, as though
the floor had revealed what it really was—
a wall fallen many years ago
when the people gave up its defense
in order to become just another city.

Holbein

Flat light like this forgives the garden
given over to riot. There was my father
waving his arms and whistling *Tales
from the Vienna Woods*. There was my mother
reduced to a bird, propped on her deathbed,
glaring in anger at all who appeared
within her ken. And my brother
the day I moaned my sourest woes
riding in his car, and his ample solicitude
and silence. A light like this one
that turned all to mugshots, as if implying
a story—Holbein's face, Van Gogh's boots—
before the ground tilted and offered
its old face to the new dusk.

The Classic Poets

It was like one of those digital movies:
I get there just in time to embrace the dead man,
already a pointillist sample or fractal
of what I remembered. When I reach in,
the spectre collapses into ropes of sand,
recoilless, and I have only myself to hug.
Aeneas' father was smoke to his arms,
while Odysseus' mother stalked the blood pail
trading prophecy for ladles.
And the mythic poet's bride,
code-named "Eurydice"
like the name of a commercial spaceship,
was confused to have found herself
summoned from a sleep of stone
only to be led blithely, as if by mistake,
toward another's dream of life.

The Apron

There's this near green and faraway blue.
The water sparkles, but not here:
that too is distant. Heidegger told me
it had a *deep limiting form*—
or was that Delmore Schwartz?
What do you do when those you love
come up from their pain, pull off their masks
and blow like whales? The whole ship
runs to one side and they're lost
in the yawing and churning where waves
and wake clash making an apron of calm
in the lap of an ironing maid.
One who knows how oils look on a wall.
Then it's on to evening.

Figures from Hardy

They walked up the hill to the spot
where the city lay before them
on the far side of the water. The slope down
was grass, then trees started up again.
The city, shapes glittering and square,
seemed a toy of clouds, which seen
from where they stood
made the sky and its events pivotal.
The rest was clumped and precious,
a Ruysdael prospect saying
that if clouds were masterly,
time was even more the faint wizard
hiding the jewels and shaking the empty cloth.
Nor were even snowdrops able
to establish their innocence,
but lined up, heads hung, like schoolchildren
who would never rise to the next form,
so brief was the light.

Steady State

Sir Fred Hoyle was going on down at the front
while we sat back—8 o'clock class—
and considered the weekend. Then he raced
from one side of the room to the other
filling the board with equations while our
professor relished his star guest,
and floor fans shouldered the air around
in our already hot room. Notwithstanding
our speaker, we knew "steady state" was bullshit,
and so we applied our patient contempt
to our general intellectual truancy
and came up short by semester's end.
The compact, nearsighted Hoyle was long
gone by that time, and the math had grown a killer.
The constellations were relegated to lab
instructed by a long-suffering planetarium assistant.
Blasé by 8, it took years to feel our own love
for the discarded, the implausible, and the romantic—
the Theory of Everything—that at twenty
never, strange to say, came into conjunction
or even made its comet graze
the outer limits of our skulls.

Skunk Cabbage

i.m. William Bronk

Once I slumped
in an Adirondack chair under an elm
in Hudson Falls, New York,
drinking the old poet's Scotch and water,
confusing the offered poems' American cubism
with the blur of the afternoon.
His never-emerging mother
sat in her room in that gabled,
porch-collared house,
but in his late fifties he was
past caring, as he was the night
the young Wakoski stiffed him
at his debut at the Y.

Yesterday, I found at last the skunk cabbage
that fed his muse blooming
in a swamp high in the mountains.
Some little bugs, as if tipped off
by the hand-cupped yellow,
self-skewered with its thick stamen,
swarmed over the bloom
with such frenzy I couldn't
look but had to push on
scrambling over roots, staying
with the marked path again,
the hard floor
unwinding among the ancient trunks.

Later by the window
leaning on sunlight, I felt
that afternoon sit quietly
with forty years, a blocked child
at the end of a bleacher row.
Now as it shifts position,
the ocean changes to that blank
metallic procession
the eye, which can barely
see anyway, finds unavoidable.

In Passing

The artist I once compared to Ulysses
who learned to chisel frowns from quarried stone,
who painted ugliness like an angel
when the art world turned from the god-hunters,
high on infinity, in favor of the urban cool
of joke and technique, died an artist's death
on the throne, midday, disappearing from
the nurse's eye into the silence of marble.

Our last visit, he emerged, gloved and rubber-
aproned, pushing his jeweler's visor bought
to disarm glaucoma, up over still-thick hair,
pausing only to point the walker more narrowly
down the ramp to his sitting room.
From there, he commenced the last lesson:
space, contour, line, stepping forth into it.
He had lost none of the manic zeal with which

years earlier he cajoled Matta into buying
a used helicopter and brought from Italy
a Roman beauty, formerly a model, and had her
dream self-creation so deep she slashed
canvas after canvas, until he showed her
how to find the ledge where space took off
and craft fell backward like a discarded barrel,
the space of the painting, I mean.

You're better than Schnabel! he thundered
at my wife, who, like a soul in Dante,

saw already the dead memory overlaid
on the old man sitting at her elbow.
She had come with her portfolio,
the student now grown powerful herself.
He urged her to study *The Last Judgment*,
that ultimate in large-scale organization.

Look at Kline, he said, *though he doesn't
go far enough*. Always the plane: *how
many dimensions to the plane?* He hurried
to answer his own question. *Depth is not
optical*, he said, *and empty depth is not
space. When things are nebulous you have
to affirm the negative with clear images.
The deeper it goes the flatter it gets.*

The negative decides the contour. Hours
of this. Weeks later, I wonder how all
the cicadas draw down their racket,
then send it spinning back through the trees,
leaving dusk to sound, night to insight
because *the negative space has to be positive.*
And because it is evening back at the stone,
a small plane passing joins the mower.

Serve You?

We were wondering whether it was better
to be the last of the old or first of the new.
Opinion was divided. M. said it was
important to carry the weight of exhaustion
as a testimony. P. concurred, adding
that the old came back anyway,
so that was moot. B. differed,
and the energy with which she invigorated
not the crumbs of the old but the dust
of the new, impressed everyone, though
some thought she was naive, possibly
immature. To press her point she tore
a page from a Fra Angelico catalogue
and used her waitress' expertise to fold it
into a napkin, which she offered to M. and P.;
"Serve you?"—like the ladies used to say
at the K&W—and danced out of the room.

Dissolve

One day in Ann Arbor, Brodsky showed me
the letter Milosz wrote him when he arrived
in America. He had written it in the Russian
that, by the by, landed him a job in the Beulah land
of California, but I don't remember any of it
beyond the greeting and summary translation
("says here he welcomes me to the U.S.").
Yet the tenor of affirmation was surrounded
by formality—the creamy stationery,
the formal return address, dead-center—
the only thing not in Cyrillic: surely
this *noblesse oblige* was irony to the exile.
Why do I remember that letter today,
now that they are both gone?
Why can't I remember the substance
of the three paragraphs, instead of
the superficial particulars and the *précis*
small enough to expand into a lone—
and in its loneliness, trite—sentence?
Where did the letter go, whose own letter
was compact with the spirit? This was
decades ago, but the rind of memory still
holds here in the chilly northwest nook
where I've made the continent's end
my pilgrimage. As evening fixes to come on
the sky is still hooked to afternoon,
though the ground is already gathering
darkness to the gardens. There is
even a cloud that looks faintly

like a whale, flukes at a slant,
swimming overhead at a great clip
out of where the sunset dissolves the day,
as if in meaning, back into how it felt.

The Pilot House

I hear a hammer down the road
sounding the wood, and inside, my daughter
at her computer making sounds half-music,
half self-amusement. The paper
on my breakfast table describes rockets
flying in and out of Israel, in and out of Lebanon.
It reminded me of that time I went home
with Teresa Greenberg, whose dad
owned the only Rolls in town.
The Six Day War had started. Her father,
a squat and burnished contractor,
rose to grunt at me and immediately
resumed his place before the console TV,
where Moshe Dayan's pirate's patch
made the good eye the focus
of our world, a world put sorely away,
an old uniform with its service medals
waiting for the grandson who could
hold the whole thing up like a chart,
telling you what each ribbon and medal
signified. Years after what might have
happened followed what did, an oil tanker
steams by, the tall pilot house seeming
to inspect the trees, then sending smoke
into the low clouds, before sailing on
to the mountains beyond the treetops.

Wised Up

It's as if some middle were erased,
the mountaintops with their peaky drifts
down which slide wrinkles of ice
but no flanks and no base: just air
pretending to be sky as if participating
in that color, that all-leveling blue.
When my philosophy professor found himself
on a panel with the Dalai Lama
what he really wanted to do, he said
was to ask him to levitate
so that he could sweep his hand under
like a kid who has wised up,
debunking the magic, finding the wires.

In the Picture

A mockingbird's tail feathers
climbed a limb. By the garbage patio
were these same feathers forcibly separated
from the body. If one were to perpetrate
some fraud, pretending hatred, say,
or boredom a whole life long,
only to recant on one's deathbed,
which would be true: that or the truth
(realizing how you leaned into
the fraud, shaded the fraud with time)?
If I awoke each morning to a mockingbird
only to find it a woodpecker in age,
wasn't the mockingbird also—
perhaps even more so—in the picture?
Wouldn't the fraud, suspending itself
over the abyss of the truth,
come to seem lovely there
in the morning of an old man?

Database

The picture an old flame sends
shows a woman with cropped hair the color
of brushed aluminum, the kind of matron
whose permission we used to seek to stay out
after the movie—and her husband, a compact
man behind a Wilford Brimley mustache.
I remember when her hair was as black
as a doctor's kit. Staring at her now, feeling
the glossy edge taking my thumbprint,
I let myself give in to a fantasy
of her easy, youthful power to achieve
or withhold a relation—whichever fit—
before a man had even realized
the lot to which he was bound
on the field where things are decided,
where one straightens into independence,
while another is unpacked as Willy Loman.
Instead there is a gray woman smiling
forward from a photo, and in her face
are years of snow and black roads. Meanwhile,
the Labrador, her other companion,
peers quizzically from her right side,
as if offering a template of companionship
straight out of a Dutch painting.
I remember our brief time years ago:
no words, but by morning that repeal
of expectation, that tectonic shift
from the brief second person back to the third.
When the boss came around, nothing,

not even a glance of camaraderie colored
her composure, as she raised her face
and proudly reported her pioneering work
on the single-member database
and the smart-list mailing program.

Only Found

I can see the first violinists sweeping the strings
and that young conductor whose choppy manner
stands in for much he has to learn from what
his hands conjure. One of my most erotic nights
occurred when I felt the thigh
of a stranger against mine at the opera.
Death and yearning alternating,
the dark act with stars sewn
to a cloth background. But when the lights
came up it was just an elderly obese woman
with nowhere else to put her legs
but in my imagination, like cake for years
in the bottom of a freezer. Such a thing
is not sought, only found: frowning faces
raising the lid, peering in.

Moulin

As I near the screen door I hear
Glenn Gould fighting his way
out of the basement, with Bach
as his stacatto commander.
I can't tell if this is for my attention
or God's, or the Gestapo's, but I find
myself thinking of the French
Resistance hero Jean Moulin
and hearing my father-in-law say,
over a candle-lit table, among guests,
how haunted he was by Moulin's refusal
to talk, even under torture. What secret,
he wondered, had no exchange value?
That made even zero, by comparison,
a safe stuffed with papers?
It was the kind of secret Bach suggested
to crazy Glenn Gould, when like a sheepdog
he dashed from side to side
on the keyboard, compressing the oxygen
of the music, until I made a clearing
for his dead master's silence
that rose up after him and squeezed
through the threshold, just as I was crossing,
going the other way.

My Street

Magritte's was no different:
streetlight's glow growing before dark
as if to usher in night and make
forgetting the thing: no fruit
suspended in air before the face
of a businessman, circa 1915,
his bowler hat as game and foolhardy
as Chaplin's; no suspect house retiring
to its daylight privacy, a locomotive
departing the hearth, heading for
even more exotic destinations than the stone
from which it emerged, puffing.
And most especially no evening air
awaiting the strollers, Strauss
swelling in tinny treble from a window
somewhere on the next orderly street.

Two Eagles

You couldn't see the head of one.
The other—higher—gripped the slight limb
like a wire cinch, its beak in profile
an oyster knife, the kind that could prise
the porcelain shell and sever the phallic muscle
in one crescent twist. I had seen them
flying at treetops earlier, and coming around the point
looked up to spy them again, receding
but no less capable of the efficient damage
we admired. Two ferries crossed, a small one
and a big. My wife and I shadowed our eyes
and went on up the beach toward the mountain.
Later as we set about to work, I heard
her start the music: Palestrina, I thought,
but well before the end I knew different.

The Missed Life

The subject was the missed life,
the one you glimpse at parties
where the brilliant doctor's gravity
pulls the room around him like a robe.
Or it could be the words breaking
over the surf of the morning paper—
her unexpected prize, his estimable death
measured in column inches, now he is gone.
One grows smaller not to have trivialized
the most cumbersome burdens.
Those years under vow, the great granite
blocks of dailiness, now thumbnails in a file.
Coleridge thought a power
moved through objects and so looking
more narrowly at the past was like
peering down the blanket to see mountains
framed in the window between your feet.
Maybe making the life one didn't have
as theme was life enough. Maybe not.
This time of year birds nest
in the monument. It was said Coleridge
knew only one man who managed completely
to live without thought of the past,
and he judged that man "a bastard."

Theology

Downstairs I hear Jill on the phone
with the oncologist. They could be
discussing theology or how to keep the strike
going without breaking the company.
After all, whole neighborhoods,
like unsecured cargo, know the rough slide
from rail to rail. She laughs

and I take it the doctor, a cautious young man,
stands momentarily in the ray
that shoots down from an opening
in the cloud cover.
Perhaps they shared a joke about age,
that party boat steaming westward
where the sun, always setting,
pokes through here and there looking,
as it were, for daylight.

Wild ducks below skim off across the sound.
Their cries answer the question
I would have put to the man,
but I see where they're going with this
and the thing, animal to animal,
they carry into the weather.

The Contest

I get detailed emails from my friends
describing events long ago. They copy
each other as the past is brought out
for another bow. They copy me,
though it's clear I haven't the memory
for the sequences, personnel, or the shading
of events, and so my contributions
are of necessity general and brief.
For all that, my memory's as stocked
as a survivalist's freezer in a '70s suburb.
I remember the tenor of particular
howls piecing the helpless air outside
beyond our open summer windows.
I recall a war once fought over a beer
that was really a spat about power,
as sex is, placed in front of justice.
And of course there was that time
my brother passed out at five,
the piss that ran circling down the chair leg
to form a puddle on the linoleum. It was
the first seizure, soon managed,
but I remember our frantic faces
as we crossed back and forth, small and dark
across his dilated pupils, the eyes
seeming not to move at all, like a contest
under way to see who was toughest,
who had the most to lose by blinking.

Big Wind

A big wind blew the Roundup
from a grassy field to my uncle's garden.
He has just finished replanting
the yellow squash and shining cucumber
and pointed out the seared leaves, drooping
but clenched, of the potato plants
he tells me will survive the fallout.
Curled edges are already giving way
to the stain of massed green, against
which defoliant can do no more
than seem insurgent. His wife is probably
losing vision in one eye; neither heart
nor lung reliable: they know the way
to the hospital. He is not sure
waking some days if his legs will
hold up his trunk, and if the garden calls,
is it in mockery? Suddenly it must seem
that much else is giving way
that was once beyond question. His sister
is moving. Living with her daughter
up in the mountains and her son-in-law,
both stubborn fundamentalists. Rush
and *Focus on the Family* will be her fare.
He wonders whether this is one
of the secret meanings of *giving*.
I remember the ease with which she posed
like Grable in a bathing suit,
my mother next to her, the farm behind,
out of focus. On the way back, an unfledged bird

stirs in the dirt on our path beneath
an old chinaberry. "Caint put it back,"
he says, looking up. "I guess
I could stomp it," he adds and peers at me
to see the effect. "But I won't."

Mastectomy

The clouds were in a frieze that day,
arabesques interlaced like a finger-church
but unable to open, sandwiched by slabs.
Like others, I waited to hear what word
there might be to divide up a future—
not the headlong, wild-hair-flying
as in the days I knew you first,
but measured and yet not less joyous
for the measuring. Milton said we are
creatures who "sigh to be renewed."
You later told how the X crossed your heart
and the surgeon described the lifting away.
Was the heart then lighter? I wanted to ask
but something overcame my impulse,
something like the moment you knew
what was dead in you was the very thing
he most had to hold precious.

Late Night

Freaks with stumps and burns.
So what if one guy had no face?
It was a program dedicated to pain,
for which reason alone it was reality
TV. The amputee described how she
let herself be spread on a website.
Cries unheard since the night my brother
drew the barrel to his brains spewed anew
from speakers like flames from the turrets
of Pandemonium, and I heard Mother
howl into the face of her young minister
again, who had raced to give her comfort.
He instead found one of the last
inscrutable secrets of his faith:
the enriching, nihilistic worship of nothing.
The reverend, a kind man who never
aimed a dart of judgment at anyone,
sat there as evening slowly toppled
into night, as the power-wire hum
of the cicadas, mad to mate and die,
amassing in the oaks and pecan trees,
overwhelmed every reason he brought
with their stern, uninflected monotony.

Immortal Soul

When the cancer rose to his brain,
my father started talking in terms
of his "immortal soul," which was unlike
the old talk of that gentle man.
One day, near the end, though wasted
to a bag twist, he went berserk
and lunged from his hospital bed
driving the nurses from the room,
as he wheeled his bed like a wagon
between himself and his tormentors.
In split-tailed hospital gown
he whirled and caught me coming
through the door. He had just
got his hand around the TV stand
and was about to pull the set,
complete with its soap opera, onto the floor,
when I stopped him. Then the look
of betrayal—so uncharacteristic—
settled in his face and hardened
the azure eyes. Taking hold of my arms
until we were locked in a struggle
like crabs dancing on the grave
of free will, he cried, "Don't you fear
for your immortal soul? Aren't you afraid?"
Finally exhausted by the manic urgency
he collapsed back into the same bed,
his wagon, taking him to the end.
Which was three days later. Rounded up
too late from a pointless meeting, I arrived

in time only to barge past the door
of the neighbor resident, an old woman
of whom I had been mostly unaware
and heard someone—a relative—who held
a picture held between them, say,
"See? It looks just like you."

Acknowledgements

The Adirondack Review, Asheville Poetry Review, AsKew Poetry Journal, The Brooklyn Rail, Café Solo, The Cortland Review, Inertia Magazine, Main Street Rag, New Literary History, Pudding Magazine, Wild Goose Poetry Review.

David Rigsbee is the author of *The Red Tower: New and Selected Poems* (2010) and seven other full-length collections. He is coeditor of *Invited Guest: An Anthology of Twentieth Century Southern Poetry* and has been the recipient of fellowships and prizes from the National Endowment for the Arts, The National Endowment for the Humanities, the Virginia Commission on the Arts, The Fine Arts Work Center in Provincetown, the Djerassi Foundation, and the Academy of American Poets.